Victim or Victor
You Always Have a Choice

Jan Payne

ISBN-13: 978-1451502466
ISBN-10: 145150246X

BISAC: Self-Help / Motivational & Inspirational
Cover and Interior Design: Attracting Possibilities

Printed in the United States of America
Victim or Victor – You Always Have a Choice
Jan Payne

ISBN-13: 978-1451502466
ISBN-10: 145150246X
1. Motivation 2. Self help. Payne, Jan. II. Title.
Victim or Victor. III. Title: You Always Have a Choice

Acknowledgement

To my mom and dad, for being a great example of marriage for over 49 years! To my dad for being Daddy Billy, for taking me to baseball games and teaching me how to throw a ball and for teaching me how to give unconditionally! To my mom for always being there, for listening, for her words of wisdom, for her grace, her charm, her yeast rolls, apple pie and for teaching me unconditional love. To my sister Ann who has been the best friend and sister a girl could ever ask for. To my son, Mike, for showing me the true meaning of love, strength and courage!

YOU always have a choice

FOREWORD

This unique book by Jan Payne is a fabulous resource and can make you *Victor*ious in life! Though it is fun and easy to read it addresses and solves a big problem that far too many people have. How you see yourself and your circumstances is crucial to success. If you think your choices are limited and that you feel like a *Victim* of circumstances and of life then you need to read and apply what is in this book. Jan proves that everyone has choices and even if your background has been tough or lacking in some way you can choose to make changes and become *Victor*ious. She shows you how to do that in a super, simple way.

If you feel that life has not been fair to you and that you are a *Victim* of less than good circumstances, bad parenting or ignorance and are constantly facing problem after problem with no end in sight this book is perfect for you. It will show you how to change everything around... and quickly.

If you want to go to the next level of success of but feel stymied or stuck this book can help you get unstuck and start moving towards that success you long for and deserve.

As an internationally recognized success expert I can say that Jan has done a great job in explaining how to get rid of the negative label of "*Victim*" and acquire a new label of "*Victor*". When you do this you will be able to achieve all your Core Desires^{tm}. **Read it NOW!**

Jack M. Zufelt
Mentor to Millions
Author of the #1 bestselling book, The DNA of
Success, International Keynote Speaker

Victim or *Victor...*

Contents

About the Author...................... **5**

Victim........................ 14

Victor........................ 26

Vague........................ 32

Visionary........................ 39

Ignorance........................ 47

Integrity........................ 51

Critical........................ 55

Creative........................ 59

Trouble – Stinkin thinkin'.................... 62

Think.................... 69

Impossible.................... 74

Optimistic.................... 80

Martyr.................... 86

Response-able.................... 89

YOU always have a choice

Puzzle Exercise 94

The Four Steps of Choice 96

Choices 97

Your Dream List 101 101

Blue Cards 106

Poems 108

P-R-O-B-E.. 112

Endorsements ....

Victim or Victor
You always have a Choice

Victim
- Vague
- Ignorance
- Critical
- Trouble
- Impossible
- Martyr

Victor
- Visionary
- Integrity
- Creative
- Thinker
- Optimistic
- Response-
  able

Be the Victor

YOU always have a choice

About the Author

Interesting how my brilliant clients -- and that includes *you* -- have affected the contents of this book – At this point I have been working with clients for over 10 years!

What I do is empower people, like **YOU** to attract possibilities. Many people call my profession Personal Success Coaching or Life Coaching. Up until a few years ago, this didn't even exist as a career!

For much of my life people would come to me and share intimate details, in an airport, on a plane or a doctor's office. Listening came so easily to me that I didn't think of it as an opportunity or a possible career. My programming was that a person should have to work hard. Now, I love what I do and I get to do it each day.

I really don't have all that many credentials if you happen to believe that degrees from universities are important. I received most of my credit hours in the mid 60's from Lesley College, a top rated teacher's school, in the heart of Harvard Square, Cambridge,

Massachusetts. My Dad always said, "That is where all nice girls go to get educated. Oh and that is also where your sister went!"

I was just 12 credit hours short of a BS degree when the love of my life decided to dump me. I became the ultimate *Victim*. After that, I took several credit hours at different colleges and universities including Cape Cod Community College, Barnstable, Massachusetts, Boston University, Boston, Massachusetts, and IBM School.

I have several certificates including one from the Gemological Institute of America.

I owned and managed Accent Jewelry, a highly successful jewelry store in a major mall from 1977-1991.

I have several certifications in the personal development world where I am currently fortunate to be connected to The Nightingale-Conant Corporation where I am recognized as an expert. In addition, I am qualified and certified to coach in the following areas.

Business Optimization - Alex Mandossian
The Science of Getting Rich, Wallace Wattles
(Certified Facilitator since 2001)
Cold Calling Success – *Victor* Antonio
Goals- Bill Bartmann, Don Hutson & Brian Tracy
Lead the Field, Earl Nightingale (also Bob Proctor- since 1998)
Think and Grow Rich, Napoleon Hill
Leverage Your Business – Jay Abraham
Negotiation – George Lucas
Personal Success Coaching and Mentoring, Brian Tracy,
Recession Proof Your Business - Brian Tracy
Relationship Intelligence – Jim Cathcart
Strategy for a Successful Business – Chet Holmes
Supercharge Your Selling - Brian Tracy,
The 10 Minute Marketers Secret Formula – Tom Feltenstein
TRUST In Teams – Stephen M.R. Covey, Boyd Matheson, Jeff Magee, Dan Clark

I have over 10 years of experience and many wonderful teachers, mentors, mastermind groups and coaches who continue to serve as resources for me.

Oftentimes, during a session with a client a question pops up that requires an answer or an explanation that I may not have a ready answer to. As if by magic, an inspirational move causes me to turn around and consult with my mastermind, my mentors, and my library! A book, a precise page and exactly the right quote, story or idea is there in front of my eyes!

Incredible! I can honestly say that the words come **to and through** me. I **know** that I am a vehicle for the message. Here is my disclaimer!

"I am not a psychiatrist or a psychologist and I don't play one on TV!"

When the idea of writing on this subject first popped into my head, I thought about the Law of Polarity. This law simply states that everything in the universe has an opposite; black/white; up/down; in/out; top/bottom; right/left... *Victim*/*Victor*!

YES!

Using an acronym for the words *Victim* and *Victor* will work!
YES!!

YOU will be able to visualize your options!

YOU always have a choice

Victim
- Vague
- Ignorance
- Critical
- Trouble
- Impossible
- Martyr

Victor
- Visionary
- Integrity
- Creative
- Thinker
- Optimistic
- Response-able

Simply look at the table and decide *if you want to be* the *Victim* or the **Victor!**

What might be a better response?

Which characteristics are **you** going to allow to surface?

My expectation is that you will use this book as a tool; that you will choose to respond rather than react and that in doing so you will improve your results.

**You always have a Choice
to Be the Victor**

Here is the original chart that I was going to use.

V	Victim; Vague	V	Victor; Visionary
I	In the dark; Igno-rant; Intimidated	I	Imaginative; Ideas; Integrity; Inspired Action; Inventive; Innovative
C	Conflicted; Competitive; Criticizes; Condemns; Complains and blames; Cynical	C	Creative; Champion; Certain Way; Conceptualizes; Considerate
T	Tentative; Troubled; Trials ad Tribulations;	T	Truth, regardless of appearance; Think; Thought; Trust
I	Immature; Impossible	O	Optimistic; Opportunity; Original; Observant; Open
M	Martyr; Magnet for Negative	R	Response-able; Resourceful; Respect; Reason

The words in this chart are great and work for the *Victor*. However, on the gazillion[th] look, I realized that it was too confusing and in fact was holding me back from getting this message to you.

Then I thought...KISS –

Keep it Super Simple!

Victim	Victor
• Vague	• Visionary
• Ignorance	• Integrity
• Critical	• Creative
• Trouble	• Thinker
• Impossible	• Optimistic
• Martyr	• Response-able

The choices were easy and the book began to write itself, to flow effortlessly!

Victim

 I believe that the *Victim* is the default mode of the universe and that it is very easy to fall into this lack, limitation and *Victim* way of life.

Victim *is Vague*
I*gnorance*
C*ritical*
T*rouble*
I*mpossible*
M*artyr*

 The polar opposite, is the **Victor**.

Victor is a **V**isionary
Integrity
Creative
Thinker
Optimistic
Response-able

Now aren't these **the** characteristics you would rather choose to exhibit on a daily basis? That's what I thought!

When Excuse or Victim mentality surfaces in a client's verbiage, I have the ability and perhaps a unique ability to detect it. People are so used to speaking that way that they don't even think about what they are saying!

I might say something like, "Is is okay with you if I reflect back to you what you just said?" When they answer affirmatively, I say, "So, what you just said is that your boss doesn't care about your situation and just keeps adding more and more work to your pile? He is such an idiot!

And you worked over 70 hours last week because the people that you work with don't do their job, so you have to do their work as well as yours?

And that you will never get it all done? And you don't get credit for it! And you didn't have any time to work on your own project because you were so busy doing everyone else's   stuff?"

Is that what you just said?" The response is often, "YES, and I don't like the way that sounds!" "WOW! I am acting like a *Victim* aren't I?"

 Isn't this a terrific little emoticon? – Here is our *Victim* under a negative cloud. Our *Victim* suffers from the 'poor me' 'oh me' or the 'why me' syndrome.

Many of us create, give energy to and live in *Victim* mentality. On a subconscious level, that is. After all, it is pretty obvious that a person wouldn't consciously choose to exhibit these qualities...

    Weak
    Powerless
    Out of control
    Loser
    Defeat

It is, however, easy to fall back into that pattern... the good news is that I am now aware of and choose to employ the tools to climb up and out sooner!

YOU always have a choice

What about you?

Have you ever played the blame game?

Recently, I saw a commercial that highlighted the negative side of society. Imagine a group of people sitting in a conference room with a huge white board. Suddenly someone says, *"Okay! Let's do some 'blame-storming!"*

This is where people talk about one and all behind their backs or complain and blame everyone for the circumstances in their lives.

WOW!

People are always blaming their circumstances for what they are. I don't believe in circumstances. The people who get on in this world are the people, who get up and look for the circumstances they want and if they can't find them, make them.
-- George Bernard Shaw

What is your role as you see it? You are after all the star of your life, the leading lady or the leading man. But are you playing the understudy, the *Victim*, or the lead role and the **Victor**?

Write your story as if you were explaining your world to someone from another planet who didn't speak your language or to a 1st or 2nd grader. What I mean is that it is best to write it in simple terms. Be sure to write what you are feeling about your current state.

Be specific, be clear and be in total integrity!

This above all: to thine own self be true, and it must follow, as the night the day, Thou canst not then be false to any man. - William Shakespeare

Are you ready?

Great!

If you are listening to this on audio format – please pause the audio and take a moment to do this exercise.

Use extra paper if you would like more room!

Did you do the exercise?

NO?

Would you rather not write in your book? That program took me a while to change. I think it stems from the fact that when I was going to elementary school we had to pass our text books in at the end of the year and if they weren't in perfect condition then we had to pay extra! It was lots of money (that is what I was told; another 'we can't afford it'…guilt)

I don't recall the amount do you? At any rate if you are still carrying around that baggage – you can choose to let it go – or…use a separate piece of paper to do any exercises!

What is your thinking? Are you playing the *Victim*? Are you one of those people who says – "Ya right – whatever? She doesn't mean me! Really – I just want to get through this book so I can say I read it!"

Believe me! I know the drill, because I used to be like you. When the program said, "Now stop the tape (oops I am dating myself; at least I didn't say 8-track!!) Or pause the CD or IPod," I would keep on listening and I just wanted to get to the next step. I truly believed that I could *'get it'* without doing the exercises or doing the work. The instructions were for everyone else...right!

You will get to **Victor** more rapidly if you do the work any of your favorite gurus have asked you to do. For sure nobody else can do this for you. Now my books look almost like coloring books. They are filled with different color highlighting and lots of notes. Yes! It feels **Victor**ious!

So now, once again, I encourage you to go back and see if you can identify a time or two when you played the *Victim.*

 Write about a time when you played the Victim.

Where do you suppose those negative thoughts originated? Well, let's talk about this for a moment.

Did you know that as a human being you are born with only two (2) fears...?

The fear of falling
The fear of loud noises

Every other fear or phobia that you have has been learned. That is the bad news. The good news is that if it has been learned... it can also be unlearned!

The key is for *you* to figure out those things, those paradigms, those habits or beliefs that were learned as 'hand me downs' that are keeping you in *Victim* mentality. So for right now, just write those phrases, those broken records that head trash that keeps repeating in your head. Get it all out! We DO become what we think about!

From birth to age 6, as human beings, we really have not yet formed a conscious awareness and so we accept uncritically from an outside source anything *anyone* tells us; sometimes referred to as *they*.

Did you ever wonder who *they* are?

My mother often said things like… "What will **they** think?" or "If we really needed it *they* would have created it already!" (*They* are… parents, teachers, siblings, relatives, friends, friends of parents, babysitters, neighbors, television, internet, entertainment, movies)

Imagine… if you will a salad bowl. Yes a simple salad bowl. What that means is that anything at all can enter and will fall in! There is no filter whatsoever!!

 In the space provided below or on a separate piece of paper, write down everything that you can think of that might be a contributing factor to your negative or Victim thinking?

Is your **SELF IMAGE** distorted?

Money is the root of all evil
I don't deserve to be rich
People won't like me
People will take it from me.
I am too young
I am too old
There nothing left for me
Rich people are snobs
People won't respect me
I am no good in crowds
I can't
People will think I have a big head
No one will come
No one wants to hear what I have to
say
Rich people cheat
I have no self esteem

Victor

 Can you see the benefits of being the *Victor?*

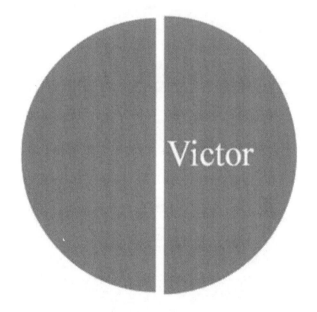

The name is of Latin origin (*Victor*is) meaning "conqueror" or "champion." It has the following connotations.

Strength
Powerful
In Control
Winner
Conqueror

 This icon respresents our '*Victor*' mentality! When you look at it don't you just want to yell "YES!!"

I believe that it is important to address the topic of success when we are talking about this subject, because the *Victim* will often complain and blame others for his lack of success.

Success most often begins with a change in the person you face in the mirror each morning! It begins inside with the decision to make great choices, no excuses and to be the *Victor*!

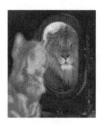

Do you see the little insecure kitty cat, the *Victim* or do YOU see little *Victim* the **mighty** lion...the **Victor**?

The Roman philosopher Epictetus once wrote,

Circumstances do not make the man.
They merely reveal him!

My desire in writing this book and sharing this with you in the simplest terms is that you will be able to utilize the **Victor** mentality more often and more rapidly!

Once you *recognize* that you are indeed in *Victim* mode, you are on your way! Awareness is the key! Once you are aware, you can then choose to *release* the *Victim* behavior and then *replace* it with your new **Victor** response!

YAHOOO!

I believe that everything begins with desire. When the desire is all consuming as in *burning desire; action and results follow!* The desire for growth! The desire to be more, do more and have more!

Desire is possibility seeking expression, or function seeking performance. – Wallace D. Wattles

Here is an acronym for desire.

Desire
• Decision
• Emotionally involved
• Secret - Your thoughs
• Imagination
• Resonate
• Energy

"D" stands for decision and the word decision comes from the Latin roots, *de* which means *from* and cedare which means – *to cut.*

"E" stands for being emotionally involved with the thing you decide you want and in this case it is the decision to become the **Victor** ☺

"S" stands for secret. And the secret is we become what we think about most of the time. Many men might say that isn't true because if it was I would be a blonde in a bikini on a beach! The truth is that if we believe we can or we believe we can't do a thing, either way we are going to be right.

"I" is for imagination. It is your ability to see yourself in possession of the good that you desire.

"R" stands for resonate – does your goal resonate with you? Are you doing this for you or for someone else? It certainly must resonate with you – at a cellular level.

"E" is for energy – give it energy and expect that you will achieve it.

On occasion, fear *of success (Victim)* is cited as a reason for lack of success. I believe that the *Victor* looks at **the** highest level or *the* highest good. Their highest level is just what they know, consciously.

Many people are afraid that when they become successful and wealthy they will lose their friends, their integrity and or their freedom. Isn't that why they wanted to get rich in the first place? FREEDOM!

Recently, there was a horrific natural disaster, a 7.0 earthquake in Haiti. Over 200,000 people were killed. I believe that each of us in our own way wanted to help.

Supermodel Gisele Bundchen donated 1.5 million dollars to The American Red Cross! Sandra Bullock, Brad Pitt and Angelina Jolie donated one million dollars to Doctors without Borders!

Wouldn't you like to be able to write a check for 1 million dollars to a cause of your choice? What a great reason to get rich! Think about the 10% you could tithe! Do the math!

Now THAT is powerful!

Vague

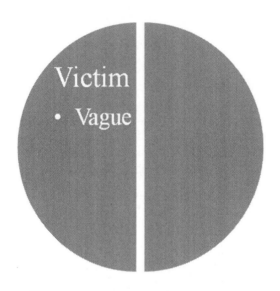

60% of the population has only a vague personal mission statement they have no road map for their lives, doing what they've always gotten without a personal life plan.

YOU always have a choice

On the *Victim* side, we have the person who is vague. The *Victim* has no direction and he is like a ship in the ocean without a rudder.

He is a wondering generality.

The *Victim*, when asked about his goals might say something like,

"I want *more* money!"
"I want to be able to do whatever I want to."
"I don't know."
"I want my "X" to do "Y"."
"I want to be happy!"
"I want a relationship"

 Do you see a problem?!

If you said these statements are too general, then you are correct! Often, the *Victim* will announce to the world that it is useless to set goals. They don't work! The truth is that the *Victim* doesn't have any specific goals. The facts support that fact that people with written goals are more successful and happy than those without written goals. I believe that this may be true because in order to write a goal, you must know what you really want.

Most *Victims* are not in control of their lives. They simply act as pawns in someone else's life. They often complain that they had something to do for someone else then later use that as a reason or an excuse for not working on their own dreams, goals or desires. This is the same person who will complain about the process of writing down goals. They will tell you it takes too much time and it just doesn't work.

"I've tried it and it doesn't work!"

"It is a waste of time."

"I never have time to work on *my* goals anyway"

There have been numerous studies done that corroborate this. When you are in love with an idea, you find a way to work on it...you give it energy every day! When there is a particular place you want to be, you find a way to get there! No matter what!

YOU always have a choice

If know what you want, know WHY you want it and know you have the WILL, the *WAY* will show up.

It is critical to be clear about what you want. It is critical to know WHY you want this thing. If your WHY is big enough you will do whatever it takes.

You may be familiar with Esther and Jerry Hicks and their book, <u>Ask and it is Given</u>. Do you think it is important to know what *it* is?

If **it** doesn't manifest then perhaps it is up to you to figure out your part in not allowing *it* to happen. In their book, they explain that everything is two things.

Either you are allowing or you are not allowing. Either you are permitting or forbidding. Which are you doing right now?

If what you want hasn't shown up yet, do you think that there is a chance you might be resisting or even forbidding the thing you want to appear?

Andrew Carnegie was very clear in conveying the message, *hidden* in the book, <u>Think and Grow Rich</u>, that each of us is born with the equivalent of two envelopes.

One marked riches and the other marked penalties... we always have a Choice!

If you DO NOT CHOOSE to USE your MIND and direct it to that which you desire; then you will be in the default mode and receive the penalties...you will be the *Victim*...

Can it be that simple? **Yes!** It is that simple!

The **Law of the Excluded Alternative** says that doing one thing means not doing something else.

A clear vision, backed by definite plans, gives you a tremendous feeling of confidence and personal power. -- Brian Tracy

 The Solution: BE clear about that which you want – Clarity is the key!

Once you know what you want and you really know **why** you want it, know you have the will (the will is one of your higher faculties and it is your ability to give yourself a directive and then follow it), the **way** will show up!

No problem can be solved until it is reduced to some simple form. The changing of a vague difficulty into a specific, concrete form is a very essential element in thinking.
- John Pierpont Morgan

No problem can be solved from the same level of consciousness that created it. Albert Einstein

Write a clear statement of what you really truly want. Remember **clarity** *is the key!*

The greater clarity you have with regard to who you are, what you want, and what you have to do to get it, the faster you will move ahead. You will accomplish much more, and your life will be better in every area. - Brian Tracy

You always have a Choice to Be the Victor

Visionary

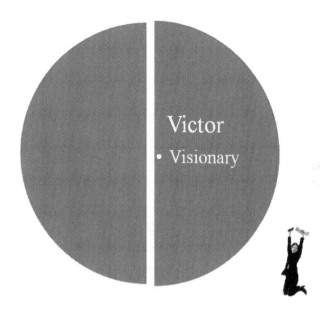

*Visionary people face the same problems
everyone else faces; but rather than get
paralyzed by their problems, visionaries
immediately commit themselves to finding a
solution. - Bill Hybels*

Visionary

The **Victor** is a Visionary. Perhaps you have heard this phrase before. Think about what you want and focus on it! When you hear that what is your reaction?

As a **Victor**, you understand this. If you think it is too much work to focus on your goal - then perhaps you might think again about what you say *you want.*

My good friend, mentor, author, speaker and mentor to millions Jack Zufelt references falling in love for the first time. Did you have to write down, gee, I better think about "X" today? You found a way to see that person and you did not have to be reminded!

 What happens to you when you look at your goal card?

YOU always have a choice

Does your heart pound to the point where you feel like it is going to POP out of your chest?

You should get really pumped and have a *burning desire* to take an action that will lead you in the direction of the completion of that thing. Do you feel ON PURPOSE?

Andrew Carnegie explained to Napoleon Hill is essential to have a *definiteness of purpose and a BURNING DESIRE!*

I recall being really passionate about the game of tennis. I loved it and would play, practice and take lessons whenever I could. My *'best friend'* (at the time) told me that I was too old to get to her level of play. I think she meant be better than or equal to her. Whenever I played her in singles, she would beat me handily and she would remind me that I was too old to ever beat her. I was around 37 yrs at the time…and *very* determined!

When I walked onto a tennis court everything changed for me. I would get excited! The endorphins would bubble up inside me. I even loved the smell of a newly opened can of tennis balls! The mention of it calls up the sound of vacuum seal breaking! Whoosh!

 I felt confident, strong and full of energy. I couldn't hit enough balls! "One more, one more volley! One more overhead! Down the line, cross court, hit it to me harder. I can take it! Make me run!"

My coach would bring me up to the net, and then hit a lob over my head, the side to side! It could be 95 degrees and it wouldn't matter. I was determined to **do** whatever was necessary to see my name on the 5.0 USTA list at the end of the season.

I would get up at the crack of dawn to take a lesson before I went to work. I would practice, practice, practice and play matches with anyone and anywhere!

Four years later, I was ranked in Colorado in singles at the 4.0 level and 2 years later moved 5.0 level! For those of you who do not play tennis, the 5.0 level is the best you can be before you are considered a 'PRO'...not only did I have a vision for what this would look like I also was willing to do whatever it took to get the trophy! I was the *Victor*!!

As a Visionary, not only do YOU know exactly what you want, you also have the ability to see yourself in possession of the good that you desire. You have the belief that you can achieve it!

In order to *achieve that which you **say you want, it is absolutely critical that you** have a **very clear picture** of that which you desire. It is, in truth the single most important thing that you can understand.

Further, it is vital that the picture is backed with emotion. Not just any emotion! *A passion; an enthusiasm; an obsession!* Andrew Carnegie said,

"A *definiteness of purpose* backed by a *burning desire.*"

Visionary

When you are obsessed and possessed with a burning desire...there are no limits to what you can or will do. You will focus easily and effortlessly! You will be on fire and on purpose!

When you are focused on what you want – all fear will disappear! YOU are the *Victor*!!

The world has a way of giving what is demanded of it. If you are frightened and look for failure and poverty, you will get failure and poverty, no matter how hard you may try to succeed.

Faith is the fuel!

*Expect **Victory** and you make **Victory**.*
Nowhere is this truer than in business life,
where bravery and faith bring both material and
spiritual rewards.
– Preston Bradley

YOU always have a choice

A pessimist is one who makes difficulties of his opportunities and an optimist is one who makes opportunities of his difficulties. --Harry Truman

Live on purpose, and work on purpose.
This vision is as important on our personal lives,
as it is in our work lives. When the two align, then
we have overall excellence.
- Steven Covey

ANYBODY can WISH
for riches, and most people do; but only a few know
that definite plans, plus a BURNING DESIRE for
wealth, are the only dependable means of
accumulating wealth. -- Napoleon Hill

You always have a Choice
to Be the Victor

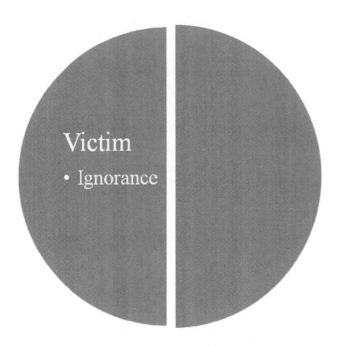

*The doorstep to the temple of wisdom is in
knowledge of our own ignorance. - Benjamin
Franklin*

Ignorance

Would a really intelligent person ever really choose ignorance?

You know, ignorance *is not bliss!* *Lack of knowledge of the law of gravity might cause one to* think *he could walk off of a 23nd story balcony and keep going. What do you* think *would happen if you walked off any balcony?*

Would it make any difference if that balcony was in Timbuktu or in New York City or in Denver, Colorado?

Would it matter how *old you were?*

Would it matter what the color of your skin or the language you speak or how *much money you have?*

Would it make any difference if you were short or tall?

YOU always have a choice

Absolutely not!

There are many other natural laws of the universe that exist. They exist whether we know about them or not.

You might hear someone say, "Oh, I didn't know that!"

Does that excuse the consequence?

Absolutely not!

To learn you need a certain degree of confidence - not too much and not too little. If you have too little confidence, you'll think you can't learn and if you have too much confidence, you will think you don't have to learn.-Eric Hoffer

Ignorance

 Write about a time when you said, "Oh, I didn't know that!"

 **Solution!** Knowledge! Knowledge alone is not power…it is *proper application of knowledge that is* potential power!

Study in your field for even fifteen minutes every single day. Whatever it is that you love! If you read even fifteen minutes a day, you will be an expert at the end of five years.

In times of change, the learners will inherit the earth while the learned will find themselves beautifully equipped to live in a world that no longer exists." – Eric Hoffer

You always have a Choice to Be the Victor

Integrity

If honesty did not exist; we would have to invent it
as the best means of getting rich - Mirabeau

The *Victor* understands the importance of Integrity in life. If we look at the word Integrity and think of it as an umbrella; then commitment, dependability, reputation, credibility and consideration would also fit under that.

Would you agree that if you are in Integrity, you would also exhibit each of those characteristics?

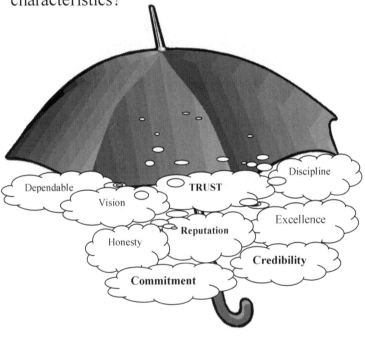

I came across this explanation of Integrity and I really like it.

Integrity comes from the Latin, which means whole or complete. A person of Integrity is honest and upright.

Many times, I hear a person say that they do not want to be successful because they will not be admired or looked up to. Does that really make any sense?

Your life only becomes better when you become better. And, Goethe said, before you can have more, you must first be more. -Brian Tracy

You always have a Choice to Be the Victor

The poverty class;
talk about and regurgitate the past.
The middle class; talk about other people.
The world class; talk about ideas!
-Steve Siebold

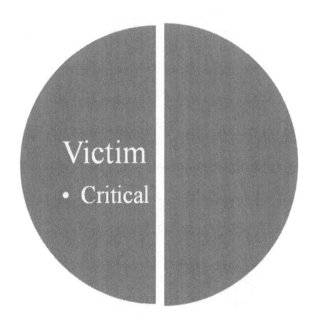

Critical

Are you a critical person?

Are you always looking for what is wrong with a situation?

Are you the kind of person who can walk into a restaurant or a shop and pick out everything that is wrong?

Are you the kind of person who will stop in the middle of a conversation to make a negative comment about someone who has just walked into the room?

You always have a Choice; you can be in *Victim mode and be the one who is constantly criticizing, complaining, condemning or blaming someone else; or you can choose to compliment*!

Do you know that some people actually thrive on conflict? They often look for any reason to find fault. Some people really enjoy being miserable.

According to Eckhart Tolle, their pain-body is looking to be fed! In The Power of Now Tolle explains how each of us has a 'pain body' that cannot be fed by joy.

It can only be fed by pain or drama and therefore many people continually look for conflict so their pain body can be fed and they can continue to be the *VICTIM!*

Drama! Drama! Drama!

I believe you can probably identify someone in your life that drains you.

When you either close the door happily behind you or hang up the phone with that person you realize how exhausted and totally drained you are!

You might choose at this moment to think about some ways that you can creatively turn that conversation around.

Think about some questions that you might be able to ask that person?

Can you change their focus in such a way that they might get caught up in the new idea and even start thinking in a new way?

next

Write a couple of questions that might change the course of your conversation.

Solution!

Choose to compliment rather than criticize. Every time you begin to criticize, take a deep breath! Imagine the sound of chalk on the blackboard. Smile! Find something good to say!

Too often we underestimate the power of a touch, a smile, a kind word, a listening ear, an honest compliment, or the smallest act of caring, all of which have the potential to turn a life around.
- Leo F. Buscaglia

You always have a Choice to Be the Victor

Creative

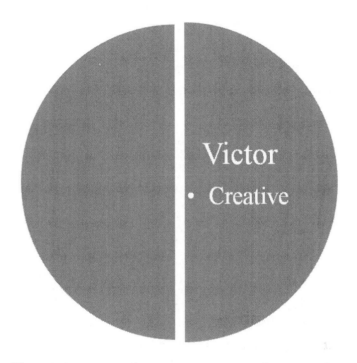

There is just as much opportunity in one business as there is in another, if only we will stop playing copycat with each other and begin thinking creatively – begin thinking in new directions.
Wallace D Wattles, The Science of Getting Rich.

When I suggest that my new clients create a habit of writing down new ideas every single day they usually don't do it. **Writing down a minimum of six new ideas each day is thinking!** It is exercising that mental muscle that has atrophied over the years from lack of use! It is said that we use less than 10% of our brain. **Most often I get comments like...**

"What do you mean?"
"What kind of new ideas?"
"I couldn't think of anything!"

In all the years I have been coaching, I have had one, only one client who successfully took on the challenge. She actually combined the process of mindstorming with the new idea concept to create 20 *new* **ideas each day.**

This particular client didn't even own a computer. She *'snail-mailed'* **the ideas to me each week, 140 new ideas each week! In that six-week period of time she created an idea for a new business, went to a library,** filled out and submitted fifteen applications for grants and received a grant and a check $300,000 to start her business.

Are you willing to take on the challenge and write down just 6 new ideas each day?

I have found that blue index cards work extremely well! Blue – why blue? The color blue activates the reticular cortex…and *that* moves you into action!

When you get a new idea it is critical to write it down! Get it on paper. The great Earl Nightingale was once quoted as saying, *Ideas are like fish, slippery little things, so you must gaff them with a pencil before they slip away*!

***You always have a Choice
to Be the Victor***

Trouble – Stinkin thinkin'

Any idea that is held in the mind; that is feared or revered; will begin at once to clothe itself in the most convenient form that is available.
- James Allen

Creative

The polar opposite of thinking is... not thinking or as Zig Ziglar calls it *stinkin' thinkin*. This characteristic of the *Victim* is where a person holds the belief that there is **TROUBLE** brewing all the time.

Do you ever find yourself thinking or saying things like, "**TROUBLE** is just around the corner!" "I wonder when the other shoe is going to drop!" "I just know that something bad is about to happen! It always does! ""Why do I always have problems?" " Why do I always run out of money?" "Why is there always more month than money?"

Once again, it is the *poor me* syndrome. Can you feel it when you say or even read those sentences? It isn't a medical term, but I think it could be! Maybe you know someone like this! Whenever something happens to the *Victim*, he/she will tell you it was the worst experience ever!

As they repeat the story over and over again, it gets worse and worse, it gets embellished. In the end it bears little or no resemblance to the original event. All the while they are giving energy to the negative. In that way they actually create their *self fulfilling prophecy of doom*... The next bad thing is sure to come to them.

One of my favorites is a story that Wayne Dyer tells. It is about his friend Bernie, who he met at the gym in Maui. One day, Bernie was sniffling, wiping his nose on his sleeve and coughing. Wayne asked him how long he had been sick. Bernie looked at him, looked at his watch, looked back at Wayne and said, "In 3 weeks it will be a month!"

I know! Can you believe it? And yet, we all know people like Bernie. Why do people buy the 1000 count of a pain reliever? Are they planning on hurting or being sick for a long period?

Here is another saying that many people use. "Get back on track!" Think about it. That track didn't work! You literally fell off it, right? So then why would you choose to get back on a track that didn't work for you?

Wouldn't you fall off that same track again sometime in the future?

Perhaps this time you ought to choose an entirely new train station to go to. Get on a brand new track. One with **definiteness of purpose;** with clarity and with a *'burning desire'*!

Take a moment and think about the last time you played the part of the *Victim*?

Is it possible that you embellished a story so that it sounded worse than it was?

What was your intention?

Is it at all possible that *you* were looking for attention?

*Write an example of an experience where you could turn that old embellished story from Victim to **Victor**!*

 **Solution!** – Create your future! Remember that your current results do not dictate your future.

You do! YOU become what you think about.

Your habitual thinking and imagery mold, fashion, and create your destiny; for as a man thinketh in his sub-conscious mind, so is he. - Dr Joseph Murphy

You always have a Choice to Be the Victor

Victim **or** *Victor...*

To believe your own thought to believe that what is true for you in your private heart is true for all men - that is genius. Yet he dismisses without notice his thought, because it is his. In every work of genius we recognize our own rejected thoughts - Ralph Waldo Emerson

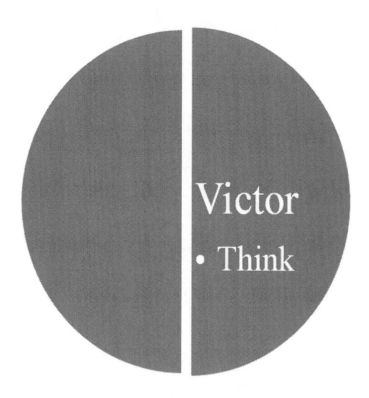

Think

Most people don't think!

If most people said what they were thinking, they would be speechless! - Earl Nightingale

*2% of the population THINKS
3% THINK they THINK
95% would rather die than THINK!
- Dr. Kenneth W. McFarland*

As a **Victor**-- you are imaginative, a **think**er and always looking for a better way. You are always asking powerful questions that lead you to powerful solutions.

*Self-discipline begins with the mastery of your thoughts.
If you don't control what you think,
you can't control what you do.
Napoleon Hill*

*Here's the key to Success and the key to failure:
We become what we think about. -
Earl Nightingale*

Did you know that it is a scientific fact that thought travels faster than the sounds of your voice? 186,000 times faster than the sound of your voice! Raymond Holliwell, in his book, <u>Working with the Law</u>; actually says this,

> *Your thought can travel from pole to pole; completely around the world in less than a single second! According to scientists, thought travels at a rate of 186,000 mile per second. That is 960,000 times faster than the sound of your voice, almost a million times faster!*

For now, suffice it to say that it truly is **your ability** *to control your thoughts to the end you desire* that determines your ability to be successful in your endeavor. That being said, you must have one particular thing... that you wish to accomplish!

If your mind is cluttered with too many things, it is like being a Jack of all trades and a master of none.

I believe that the missing secret is simply the realization that it is essential to use your ability to control, focus and concentrate your thoughts. That is important because thoughts are things – they have wings!

If you do **not** choose to control those thoughts *(and it is a choice to do that☺...)* it is very likely that you will get the scraps, the penalties, the lack and limitation!

If you aren't consciously thinking and focusing on a thing that you want…then other's thoughts penetrate your mind and you will accept uncritically what they send to you. The *Victor* is a thinker and understands the power of thought!

Wallace D. Wattles wrote <u>The Science of Getting Rich</u> in 1903 and published it in 1910 and in it we find this incredible passage repeated nine times!

There is a thinking stuff from which all things are made
and which in its original state
permeates, penetrates and fills the interspaces of the universe

A thought held in this substance
produces the thing that is imaged by the thought.

I can form things in my thought
and by impressing my thought on the formless
substance
can cause the thing I think about to be created.

Thought or think is mentioned 212 times in this book and also 220 times in Napoleon Hill's classic, Think and Grow Rich.

One time at a seminar the keynote speaker asked, "How many of you have read Think and Grow Rich?" About 95% of the people in the room raised their hands. Then he followed that with another question. "How many of you are rich?" About 3 people raised their hands! Addressing the rest of the audience, he said, "You got the think part down didn't you?" Most of the audience laughed, but the truth is that they didn't get the **think** part down, because if they did, they would be rich!

In their poem Stuart and Edward White talk about how one day, something happens that literally stops you in your tracks and you get it. The *Victor* gets it!

It is like a sudden explosion!

BOOM!

Many clients experience a *shift* – this is no little shift. It is a **giant awareness!** A step up in consciousness! A new level of thinking!

YAHOOO!

Whatever we are waiting for - peace of mind, contentment, grace, the inner awareness of simple abundance - it will surely come to us, but only when we are ready to receive it with an open and grateful heart.-- Sarah Ban Breathnach

You always have a Choice to Be the Victor

Impossible

A story that is told in the classic success book, <u>Think and Grow Rich</u> is of Henry Ford's vision of the modern 8-cylinder motor.

He called his engineers, told them of his idea, and asked them to design it.

They came back to him with the bad news.

"Impossible"!

Ford said, "Try Again"!

This went on for some time-

Impossible! Try Again! Impossible! Try Again!

You already know the ultimate outcome. You might even have one under the hood of the car in your driveway! - Napoleon Hill

Impossible!

How!

Both of these words when used in this way can be considered a complete sentence!

How? When it is used like that as a question, I believe that it causes the *Victim* mentality to surface. The *Victim* sees things as they are and continues to believe these conditions cannot be changed. The word how is prevalent in their vocabulary –When a person asks, "how?" It is whiny and worrisome and coveys impossible!

For example, how in the world am I ever going to get this done? Or how can I achieve that goal? Or how can I get "X" when I don't have any "Y"?

If you believe that something is impossible and that there is no way it can be done, you will be right.

Henry Ford said it best,
If you believe you can or you believe you can't
either way you will be right!

Many of the people in our society have been brought up to believe that the following things are true:

New things are not possible.

Everything we need is already here

We really do not need anything else

There can't be anything new...if it was necessary it would already be here...they would have created it!

In a study done at Harvard University in the late 50's or early 60's, it was concluded that by the time we reach the age of twenty-one, 75% of our thinking is negative and working against us! Zig Ziglar calls it stinkin' thinkin!

Is it any wonder that we get intimidated and believe that a thing is impossible? If you focus on the negative, what do you think you are going to attract? RIGHT!! More negative!

What can you do to change your thinking from impossible to probable?

Solution! Ask questions that will open up the channels of possibilities like...

What are the ways that I can do "X"?

Wouldn't it be nice IF...?

Do you feel the difference?

Try it on for size! Don't you feel a sense of freedom? And wouldn't you agree that the ideas, options and possibilities begin to flow? Don't you feel open to opportunities and lighter! **YAHOOO!!**

> *You always have a Choice*
> *to Be the Victor*

Optimistic

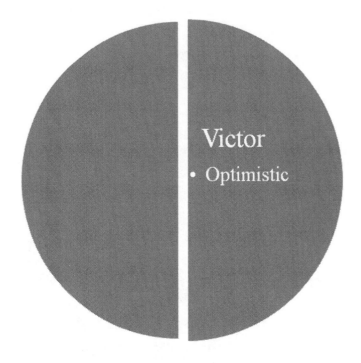

I wake up feeling that the impossible means nothing-there is no limits, have no fears & of course: reach for the unreachable. – **Apolo Anton Ohno**, *Olympic Gold Medal Winner*

YOU always have a choice

Being optimistic is a critical characteristic of the *Victor*! When you expect the best, you get the best.

What would your life be like if you got up every morning believing that everyone in the world was there to help you get whatever you wanted?

Can you begin to imagine how wonderful it would be if every time you stepped outside your comfort zone there would be hoards people waiting to lift you up, support you in every move and act as a proverbial safety net!

When you expect the best, you look for the good things. You are what I call a *good finder*!

This is different from a Pollyanna.

The optimist prepares for the worst and expects the best. When something bad happens, the *Victor* knows which tools to use to find solutions.

Optimistic

The optimistic person believes that he or she can truly make a difference.

What about you?

Do you really believe that **you** can make a difference?

Did you ever hear the story of a young boy standing on the shore and throwing star fish back into the ocean?

Story of the Starfish!

Once upon a time, an old man was walking along a beach. The sun was shining and it was a beautiful day. Off in the distance he could see a child going back and forth between the surf's edge and the beach...

As the old man approached he could see that there were hundreds of starfish stranded on the sand as the result of a recent storm.

The old man was stuck by the apparent futility of the task. There were far too many starfish.
Many of them were sure to perish.

YOU always have a choice

As he approached the little boy continued the task of picking up starfish one by one and throwing them into the surf.

As he came up to the little boy, he said, "You must be crazy. There are thousands of miles of beach covered with starfish.

You can't possibly make a difference. The little boy looked at the old man.

He then stooped down and picked up one more starfish and threw it back into the ocean.

He turned back to the old man and said,

It sure made a difference to that one!

Optimistic

When you are optimistic, you are confident that an event will turn out right. Many people use so much energy expecting the worst. As an optimistic person and a *Victor*, you learn to redirect or transmute your energy into positive expectation!

*You always have a Choice
to Be the Victor*

You must take personal responsibility. You cannot change the circumstances, the seasons or the winds, but you can change yourself.-Jim Rohn

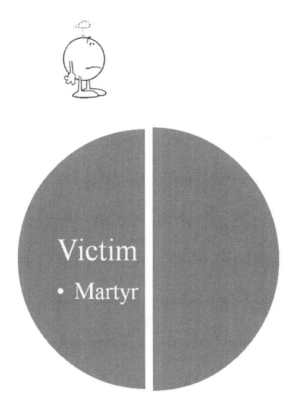

Martyr

The *Victim* reacts and is a MARTYR AND A MAGNET FOR THE NEGATIVE. How does that sound to you? Not so good? What about you?

Do you ever say anything like, "That's okay?

There is no need for you to worry about a thing! I'll do it."

"No, you don't have worry about it! I can deal with it!"

"Never mind, I'll do it myself!"

The *Victim* is a martyr and will often look for reasons to complain about the very thing that they offered to do.

They will be the person who pops in to handle a family situation and then later complain that no one else in the family ever does anything.

Then they will grumble about the fact that they didn't get a chance to make that very important phone call.

They may relate the story to you in a way that implies they were *victim*ized, they had no choice and they feel good because they helped out someone else.

Anyway, they felt needed and useful in an otherwise 'useless' or undirected day.

 *Solution!* If this is you, choose to change! Find your "NO!" The word no is a complete sentence! It is! There is no need to explain. It is not necessary to find some kind of an excuse!

Write an example of a conversation where you can use NO comfortably!

**You always have a Choice
Be the Victor**

Response-able

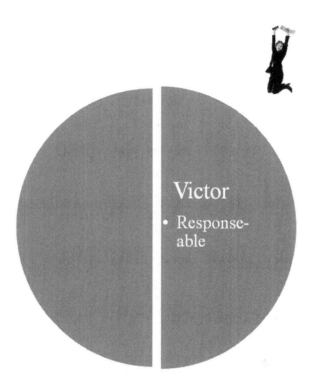

*Ultimately, man should not ask what the meaning of his life is, but rather must recognize that it is he who is asked. In a word, each man is questioned by life; and he can only answer to life by answering for his own life; to life he can only respond by being responsible. - **Victor Frank***

Response-able

The *Victor* always takes responsibility! What exactly does response-able mean to you?

 Write your definition of response-able here.

When we separate the syllables in this word – we get two very important words, response plus ability. It is your ability to respond rather than react to any particular event. It is the highest level of consciousness; mastery.

The *Victor* is aware! The *Victor* responds!
YOU are the Victor!

Response-able

I am responsible for my life;
I am responsible for my health
I am responsible for my wealth,
***I am responsible** for my happiness,*
***I am responsible** for my relationships,*
***I am responsible** for my fitness,*
***I am responsible** for controlling my mind*
- to ends that I desire,
***I am responsible** for my spirituality*
***I am responsible** for every result I get.*

Signature	Date

Victim or *Victor...*

Victim	Victor
• Vague	• Visionary
• Ignorance	• Integrity
• Critical	• Creative
• Trouble	• Thinker
• Impossible	• Optimistic
• Martyr	• Response-able

You always have a Choice
Be the Victor

Tools

Puzzle Exercise

Part I

Turn all pieces of the puzzle upside down – put the cover away – no color and no picture. Spend 10 minutes – **no more than 10 minutes** putting the puzzle together without the cover and without turning the pieces over to see if the color is right.

 Write your feelings here!

Part II

Turn all pieces of the puzzle right side up –
get the cover. Spend 10 minutes – **no more
than 10 minutes** putting the puzzle together
with the colors showing and with the picture
n the cover.

 Write your feelings here!

The Four Steps of Choice

The Four Steps of Choice

1. Say to yourself (or out loud if you want to),

"IS THIS A CHOICE?"

2. If the answer is yes, then immediately say to yourself,

"THIS CHOICE IS MINE."

3. Next, as soon as you have given the Choice as much or as little thought as it requires consciously say or think to yourself the words...

"MY CHOICE IS . . ."

4. Always be aware at a conscious level of why you have made the Choice.

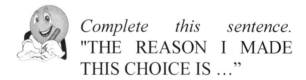 *Complete this sentence.* "THE REASON I MADE THIS CHOICE IS ..."

The Four Steps of Choice

Your birth certificate doesn't come with any guarantees of great success, but at birth you do come fully equipped with certain talents and abilities, desires and choices -Jack M. Zufelt

Choices

Any of you who have been through the coaching process with me know how important 'what you say to yourself' is. Shad Helmstetter wrote a wonderful book which is titled, **What to Say When You Talk to Yourself.** I find myself quoting him quite often.

There is a wonderful story that I like to share from another book of his called **Choices**. In the introduction, Shad tells a story that got my attention. It was so touching that I wrote to Shad and asked permission to use this information so that you all could benefit from it. He emailed me and said that it would be fine!

He tells the story of infants twins wrapped in blankets and left on the steps of a palace. Their names were Naci and T'Naci. The birth mother left them with a gift. The gift was wrapped in a small cloth and written on the cloth were these words.

This is the only gift, beyond my love for you that I can give you. Take it and when it is time, use this gift to create the life I would have wished for you

YOU always have a choice

Chose right from wrong	
I always do my best to choose right from wrong	I do not always do my best to choose right from wrong

Choose to work for what you believe in	
I choose to work for what I believe in	I do not choose to work for what I believe in

Choose to make decisions for your own actions	
I choose to make decision for myself	I do not choose to make decisions for myself

Choose Your Goal and Decision	
I have chosen my goal and direction	I have not chosen my goal and direction

Choose to love and be loved	
I choose to love and be loved	I do not choose to love and be loved

Choose to choose every detail of your life	
I choose every detail of my life	I do not choose every detail of my life

Victim or *Victor*...

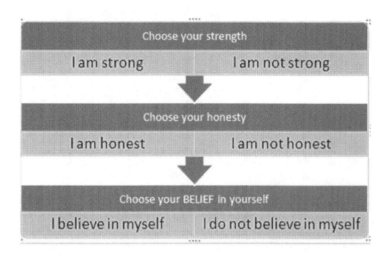

Your Dream List 101

1	
2	
3	
4	
5	
6	
7	
8	
9	
10	
11	
12	
13	
14	
15	
16	
17	
18	
19	
20	
21	
22	
23	
24	
25	

Keep Going!

26	
27	
28	
29	
30	
31	
32	
33	
34	
35	
36	
37	
38	
39	
40	
41	
42	
43	
44	
45	
46	
47	
48	
49	
50	

Keep Going!

51	
52	
53	
54	
55	
56	
57	
58	
59	
60	
61	
62	
63	
64	
65	
66	
67	
68	
69	
70	
71	
72	
73	
74	
75	

Almost There!

76	
77	
78	
79	
80	
81	
82	
83	
84	
85	
86	
87	
88	
89	
90	
91	
92	
93	
94	
95	
96	
97	
98	
99	
100	

One more!

CONGRATULATIONS!!

YOU did it!!

This is a great exercise that *the* **Victor**
(*Mr. or Ms.* **Success**)
does quarterly or more!

Blue Cards

 6 New Ideas Everyday!
You won't love every idea, but when you find something you really want more than anything, the next step is to take action.

My New Ideas

Blue activates your reticular cortex!

Often the difference between a successful person and a failure is not the one that has better abilities or ideas, but the courage that one has to bet on one's ideas, to take a calculated risk - and to act.
- Dr. Maxwell Maltz

DO IT NOW!

It is critical to be in love with whatever you decide to do. It must be the driving force! When you have that driving force nothing and I mean nothing will stand in your way. That thing that you want should scare you and excite you at the same time! Think about what your life will be like when you achieve this!

I ask not for more riches; but for more wisdom with which to accept and use wisely; the riches I received at birth; in the form of the power to control my own mind; to whatever ends I desire.
-Napoleon Hill

Poems

If you think you are beaten
Walter D. Wintle

YOU CAN if you think you can!
If you think you are beaten, you are,
If you think you dare not, you don't
If you like to win, but you think you can't,
It is almost certain you won't

If you think you'll lose, you're lost
For out of the world we find,
Success begins with a fellow's will—
It's all in the state of mind.

If you think you are outclassed, you are,
You've got to think high to rise,
You've got to be sure of yourself before
You can ever win a prize.

Life's battles don't always go
To the stronger or faster man,
But soon or late the man who wins
Is the man WHO THINKS HE CAN!

Poems

Wisdom
Stewart Edward White and Harwood White

Curious how we acquire wisdom
Over and over again,
the same truth is thrust under our very noses.
We encounter it in action; we are admonished of it;
we read it in the written word.
We suffer the experience; we gradually assent to the
advice; we approve, intellectually, the written word.
But nothing happens inside us.

Then, one day, some trivial experience or word or
encounter stops us short.
A gleam of illumination penetrates
the depth of our consciousness.
We see!
Usually it is but a glimpse; but on rare occasions a
brilliant flash reveals truth fully formed.
And we marvel that this understanding has escaped
us so long.

One and Only You
James T. Moore

Every single blade of grass,
And every flake of snow—
Is just a wee bit different,
There's no two alike, you know.

From something small, like grains of sand,
To each gigantic star
All were made with THIS in mind:
To be just what they are!

How foolish then, to imitate—
How useless to pretend!
Since each of us comes from a MIND
Whose ideas never end.

There'll only be just ONE of ME
To show what I can do
And you should likewise feel very proud,
There's only ONE of YOU.

Poems

Thoughts are Things
by Ella Wheeler Wilcox

I hold it true that thoughts are things;
They're endowed with bodies
and breath and wings:

And that we send them forth to fill
The world with good results, or ill.

That which we call our secret thought
Speeds forth to earth's remotest spot

Leaving its blessings or its woes;
like tracks behind it as it goes.

We build our future, thought by thought,
For good or ill, yet know it not.

Yet so the universe was wrought.
Thought is another name for fate

Choose then thy destiny and wait
for love brings love and hate bri

P-R-O-B-E

First, what is your **P**erception or your programming relative to "X"?

Second, is that still **R**eal?

Third, is this belief **O**bsolete?

Fourth, is this belief excess **B**aggage?

Fifth, **E**rase and replace it!

 *Remember that if we do not replace a bad behavior with a good behavior, we will, by law replace it with another bad behavior. Nature abhors a vacuum. So then what is a possible thought or action you could replace this old program with?*

Recognize; Release; Replace!

Endorsements

"This is a vital concept for success and happiness. This enjoyable, insightful book shows you the secret to taking complete control over your emotions and your life. It moves you from power-less to power-full in one giant step."

Brian Tracy, author 47 books including GOALS and Maximum *Achievement*

*"You want to be a **Victor** and not a Victim. This book shows you how to stop the cycle of Victimhood and step into the greatness that lies inside you."*

Noah St. John, author *The Secret Code of Success;* Inventor of AFFORMATIONS

*"Happiness belongs to the **VICTOR**; this book will show you how to choose **Victor** as your default position."*

Edwin Edebiri, Chief Happiness Officer, I Am Happy Project

*"This book explains how to get rid of the negative label of "Victim" and acquire a new label of "**Victor!**" When you do this you will be able to achieve all your Core Desires™."*

Jack M. Zufelt, author The *DNA of Success*

YOU
are the
VICTOR!

Made in the USA
Charleston, SC
05 December 2015